SOCIETAS

essays in political and cultural criticism

2007–2008

Societas: Essays in Political and Cultural Criticism

Public debate has been impoverished by two competing trends. On the one hand the trivialization of the media means that in-depth commentary has given way to the ten-second soundbite. On the other hand the explosion of knowledge has increased specialization, and academic discourse is no longer comprehensible.

This was not always so, especially for political debate, but in recent years the tradition of the political pamphlet has declined, as publishers found that short books were uneconomic. However the introduction of the digital press makes it possible to re-create a more exciting age of publishing. *Societas* authors are all experts in their own field, but these accessible essays are written for a general audience.

The books are available retail at the price of £8.95/$17.90 from your local bookshop, or using the order form in the main Imprint Academic catalogue, or online at imprint-academic.com/books. However you can obtain the current volume on bi-monthly subscription for £5/$10 (back volumes only **£2.50** each for new subscribers), using the Direct Debit form on the back cover of this pamphlet. Details and updates at **imprint-academic.com/societas**

The Right Road to Radical Freedom

Tibor R. Machan

The Right Road to
Radical Freedom

Tibor R. Machan

This work focuses on the topic of freedom. The author starts with the old issue of free will – do we as individual human beings choose our conduct, at least partly independently, freely? He comes down on the side of libertarians who answer Yes, and scorns the compatibilism of philosophers like Daniel Dennett, who try to rescue some kind of freedom from a physically determined universe. From here he moves on to apply his belief in radical freedom to areas of life such as religion, politics, and morality, tackling subjects as diverse as taxation, private property, justice and the welfare state.

Tibor Machan is no mere theoretician. He was smuggled out of Hungary in 1953, as a 14-year old, and served in the US Air Force before taking up academic life. He has written many books and presents his robust views in a trenchant no-nonsense style. The author teaches ethics at Chapman University and is a research fellow at Stanford University's Hoover Institution.

128 pp., £8.95/$17.90, 9781845400187 (pbk.), January 2007, *Societas,* Vol.26

Paradoxes of Power: Reflections on the Thatcher Interlude

Sir Alfred Sherman (1919-2006)

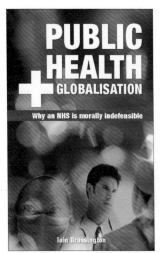

Thumb through the index of any study of the Thatcher years and you will come across the name of Sir Alfred Sherman. In her memoirs Lady Thatcher herself pays tribute to his 'brilliance', the 'force and clarity of his mind', his 'breadth of reading and his skills as a ruthless polemicist'. She credits him with a central role in her achievements.

Born in 1919 in London's East End, until 1948 Sherman was a Communist and fought in the Spanish Civil War. But he ended up a free-market crusader. Sherman examines the origins and development of 'Thatcherism', but concludes that it was an 'interlude' and that the post-war consensus remains largely unscathed.

'These reflections by Thatcherism's inventor are necessary reading.'
Sir John Hoskyns, *Salisbury Review*

'This book should be read by anyone examining this period.' **Margaret Thatcher**

'These essays are highly relevant to the politics of today.' **Norman Tebbit**

'Sherman suplied much of the drive to turn back the tide of collectivism.' *Guardian*

'Sherman made a crucial and beneficient contribution to modern Britain.' *Independent*

edited by Mark Garnett, University of Lancaster
200 pp., £8.95/$17.90, 9781845400927 (pbk.), March 2007, *Societas*, Vol.27

Public Health & Globalisation

by Iain Brassington

This book claims that the NHS is morally indefensible. There is a good moral case in favour of a *public* health service, but these arguments do not point towards a *national* health service, but to something that looks far more like a *transnational* health service.

Drawing on Peter Singer's famous arguments in favour of a duty of rescue, the author, who lectures in law at Manchester University argues that the cost of the NHS is unjustifiable. If we accept a duty to save lives when the required sacrifice is small, then we ought also to accept sacrifices in the NHS in favour of foreign aid. This does not imply that the NHS is wrong; just that it is hard to justify speding thousands of pounds on one person in Britain when the money could save many more lives elsewhere.

96 pp., £8.95/$17.90, 9781845400798 (pbk.), May 2007, *Societas*, Vol.28

Why Spirituality is Difficult for Westerners

David Hay

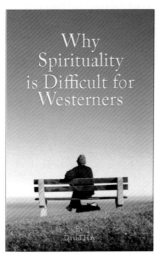

A zoologist by profession, David Hay holds that religious or spiritual awareness is biologically natural to the human species and has been selected for in organic evolution because it has survival value. Although naturalistic, this hypothesis is not intended to be reductionist with regard to religion. Indeed, it implies that all people, even those who profess no religious belief, nonetheless have a spiritual life.

This book documents the repudiation of religion in the West, describes the historical and economic context of European secularism, and considers recent developments in our understanding of the neurophysiology of the brain as it relates to religious experience.

Dr Hay is Honorary Senior Research Fellow at the University of Aberdeen.

96 pp., £8.95/$17.90, 9781845400484 (pbk.), July 2007, *Societas*, Vol.29

Earthy Realism: The Meaning of GAIA

Mary Midgley (ed.), James Lovelock (foreword)

GAIA, named after the ancient Greek mother-goddess, is the notion that the Earth and the life on it form an active, self-maintaining whole. By its use of personification it attacks the view that the physical world is inert and lifeless.

It has a *scientific* side, as shown by the new university departments of earth science which bring biology and geology together to study the continuity of the cycle. It also has a visionary or *spiritual* aspect. What the contributors to this book believe is needed is to bring these two angles together. With global warming now an accepted fact, the lessons of GAIA have never been more relevant and urgent.

Contributors include James Lovelock, Mary Midgley, Richard Betts, Susan Canney, Maggie Gee, Brian Goodwin, Stephan Harding, John Mead, David Midgley, Anne Primavesi, Joan Solomon, Pat Spallone, John Turnbull, David Wilkinson and John Ziman.

Mary Midgley is a philosopher with an interest in relations between humans and the rest of nature (especially animals), in the sources of morality, and in the tendency of 'scientism' to become a religion.

120 pp., £8.95/$17.90, 9781845400804 (pbk.), Sept. 2007, *Societas*, Vol.30

Joseph Conrad Today
Kieron O'Hara

This book argues that the novelist Joseph Conrad's work speaks directly to us in a way that none of his contemporaries can. Conrad's scepticism, pessimism, emphasis on the importance and fragility of community, and the difficulties of escaping our history are important tools for understanding the political world in which we live. He is prepared to face a future where progress is not inevitable, where actions have unintended consequences, and where we cannot know the contexts in which we act.

Heart of Darkness uncovers the rotten core of the Eurocentric myth of imperialism as a way of bringing enlightenment to 'native peoples' – lessons which are relevant once more as the Iraq debacle has undermined the claims of liberal democracy to universal significance.

The result can hardly be called a political programme, but Conrad's work is clearly suggestive of a sceptical conservatism of the sort described by the author in his 2005 book *After Blair: Conservatism Beyond Thatcher*. The difficult part of a Conradian philosophy is the profundity of his pessimism – far greater than Oakeshott, with whom Conrad does share some similarities (though closer to a conservative politician like Salisbury). Conrad's work poses the question of how far we as a society are prepared to face the consequences of our ignorance.

96 pp., £8.95/$17.90, 9781845400668 (pbk.), Nov. 2007, *Societas,* Vol.31

Who Holds the Moral High Ground?
Colin J Beckley and Elspeth Waters

Meta-ethical attempts to define concepts such as 'goodness', 'right and wrong', 'ought' and 'ought not', have proved largely futile, even over-ambitious. Morality, it is argued, should therefore be directed primarily at the reduction of suffering, principally because the latter is more easily recognisable and accords with an objective view and requirements of the human condition. All traditional and contemporary perspectives are without suitable criteria for evaluating moral dilemmas and without such guidance we face the potent threat of sliding to a destructive moral nihilism. This book presents a possible set of defining characteristics for the foundation of future moral evaluations and engagements, taking into consideration that the historically maligned female gender may be better disposed to ethical leadership.

96 pp., £8.95/$17.90, 9781845401030 (pbk.), January 2008, *Societas,* Vol.32

Froude Today
John Coleman

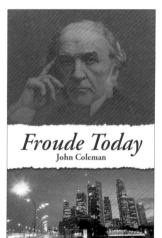

A.L. Rowse called fellow-historian James Anthony Froude the 'last great Victorian awaiting revival'. The question of power is the problem that perplexes every age: in his historical works Froude examined how it applied to the Tudor period, and defended Carlyle against the charge that he held the doctrine that 'Might is Right'.

Froude applied his analysis of power to the political classes of his own time and that is why his writings are just as relevant today. The historian and the prophet look into the inner meaning of events – and that is precisely what Froude did – and so are able to make judgments which apply to ages far beyond their own. The last chapters imagine what Froude would have said had he been here today.

120 pp., £8.95/$17.90, 9781845401047 (pbk.), March 2008, *Societas,* Vol.33

The Enemies of Progress
Austin Williams

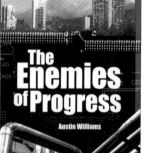

This polemical book examines the concept of sustainability and presents a critical exploration of its all-pervasive influence on society, arguing that sustainability, manifested in several guises, represents a pernicious and corrosive doctrine that has survived primarily because there seems to be no alternative to its canon: in effect, its bi-partisan appeal has depressed critical engagement and neutered politics.

It is a malign philosophy of misanthropy, low aspirations and restraint. This book argues for a destruction of the mantra of sustainability, removing its unthinking status as orthodoxy, and for the reinstatement of the notions of development, progress, experimentation and ambition in its place.

Al Gore insists that the 'debate is over'. while musician K.T. Tunstall, spokesperson for 'Global Cool', a campaign to get stars to minimize their carbon footprint, says 'so many people are getting involved that it is becoming really quite uncool *not* to be involved'. This book will say that it might not be cool, but it is imperative to argue against the moralizing of politics so that we can start to unpick the contemporary world of restrictive, sustainable practices.

The author is the director of the **Future Cities Project** and tutor at the Royal College of Art and Bartlett School of Architecture and the Built Environment.

96 pp., £8.95/$17.90, 9781845400989 (pbk.), May 2008, *Societas,* Vol.34

Debating Humanism

Dolan Cummings (ed.)

More than to sleep and feed, to be human is to debate, to argue and to engage with the ideas and opinions of others. And a recurring theme is the very question of what it means to be human, and the nature of our relationship to the world, to each other and to gods or God. This has never been an idle debate: it is intimately bound up with how society is organised and where authority lies. Broadly speaking, the humanist tradition is one in which it is we as human beings who decide for ourselves what is best for us, and are responsible for shaping our own societies. For humanists, then, debate is all the more important, not least at a time when there is much discussion about the unexpected return of religion as a political force determining how we should live.

This collection of essays follows the Institute of Ideas' inaugural Battle of Ideas festival at the Royal College of Art in London in October 2005. Contributors include Josie Appleton, Simon Blackburn, Robert Brecher, Andrew Copson, Dylan Evans, Revd. Anthony Freeman, Frank Furedi, A.C. Grayling, Dennis Hayes, Elisabeth Lasch-Quinn, Kenan Malik and Daphne Patai.

96 pp., £8.95 / $17.90, 9781845400699 (pbk.), *Societas,* Vol.25

Village Democracy

John Papworth

'A civilisation that genuinely reflects all that human beings long for and aspire to can only be created on the basis of each person's freely acknowledged power to decide on each of the many questions that affect his life.' In the forty years since he wrote those words in the first issue of his journal *Resurgence*, John Papworth has not wavered from that belief. This latest book passionately restates his argument for radical decentralisation as the only answer to the current crises in politics, trade, ecology and international affairs.

Revd. John Papworth is founding editor of *Resurgence* and *Fourth World Review*. His many books including *Small Is Powerful*.

'If we are to stand any chance of surviving we need to heed Papworth's call for decentralisation'
Zac Goldsmith, *The Ecologist*

'If anything will save this world and in time enough, it will be the insightfulness and wisdom John Papworth displays in this little volume.' **Kirkpatrick Sale**

96 pp., £8.95 / $17.90, 9781845400644 (pbk.), *Societas,* Vol.24

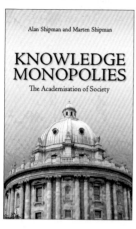

Knowledge Monopolies
Alan Shipman & Marten Shipman

Historians and sociologists chart the *consequences* of the expansion of knowledge; philosophers of science examine the *causes*. This book bridges the gap. The focus is on the paradox whereby, as the general public becomes better educated to live and work with knowledge, the 'academy' increases its intellectual distance, so that the nature of reality becomes more rather than less obscure.

'A deep and searching look at the successes and failures of higher education.' *Commonwealth Lawyer*

'A must read.' *Public* (The Guardian)

£8.95/$17.90, 9781845400286 (pbk), *Societas* V.20

The Referendum Roundabout
Kieron O'Hara

A lively and sharp critique of the role of the referendum in modern British politics. The 1975 vote on Europe is the lens to focus the subject, and the controversy over the referendum on the European constitution is also in the author's sights.

The author is a senior research fellow at the University of Southampton and author of *Plato and the Internet*, *Trust: From Socrates to Spin* and *After Blair: Conservatism Beyond Thatcher* (2005).

£8.95/$17.90, 9781845400408 (pbk), *Societas* V.21

The Moral Mind
Henry Haslam

The reality and validity of the moral sense took a battering in the last century. Materialist trends in philosophy, the decline in religious faith, and a loosening of traditional moral constraints added up to a shift in public attitudes, leaving many people aware of a questioning of moral claims and uneasy with a world that has no place for the morality. Haslam shows how important the moral sense is to the human personality and exposes the weakness in much current thinking that suggests otherwise.

'Marking a true advance in the discussion of evolutionary explanations of morality, this book is highly recommended for all collections.' **David Gordon**, *Library Journal*

'An extremely sensible little book. It says things that are really rather obvious, but which have somehow got forgotten.' **Mary Midgley**

£8.95/$17.90, 9781845400163 (pbk), *Societas* V.22

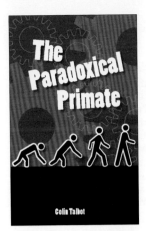

The Paradoxical Primate
Colin Talbot

This book seeks to explain how human beings can be so malleable, yet have an inherited set of instincts. When E.O. Wilson's *Consilience* made a plea for greater integration, it was assumed that the traffic would be from physical to human science. Talbot reverses this assumption and reviews some of the most innovative developments in evolutionary psychology, ethology and behavioural genetics.

'Talbot's ambition is admirable…a framework that can simultaneously encompass individualism and concern for collective wellbeing.' *Public* (The Guardian)

£8.95/$17.90, 9780907845850 (pbk), *Societas* V.14

Putting Morality Back Into Politics
Richard D. Ryder

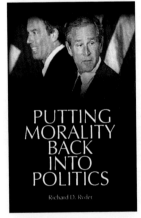

Ryder argues that the time has come for public policies to be seen to be based upon moral objectives. Politicians should be expected routinely to justify their policies with open moral argument. In Part I, Ryder sketches an overview of contemporary political philosophy as it relates to the moral basis for politics, and Part 2 suggests a way of putting morality back into politics, along with a clearer emphasis upon scientific evidence.

Trained as a psychologist, Ryder has also been a political lobbyist, mostly in relation to animal welfare.

£8.95/$17.90, 9781845400477 (pbk), *Societas* V.23

Tony Blair and the Ideal Type
J.H. Grainger

The 'ideal type' is Max Weber's hypothetical leading democratic politician, whom the author finds realized in Tony Blair. He is a politician emerging from no obvious mould, treading no well-beaten path to high office, and having few affinities of tone, character or style with his predecessors. He is the Outsider or Intruder, not belonging to the 'given' of British politics and dedicated to its transformation. (The principles outlined are also applicable. across the parties, in the post-Blair period.) The author was reader in political science at the Australian National University and is the author of *Character and Style in English Politics* (CUP).

'A brilliant essay.' **Simon Jenkins**, *Sunday Times*
'A scintillating case of the higher rudeness.' *Guardian*
£8.95/$17.90, 9781845400248 (pbk), *Societas* V.15

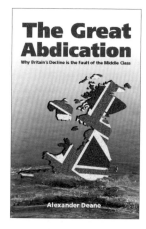

The Great Abdication
Alex Deane

According to Deane, Britain's middle class has abstained from its responsibility to uphold societal values, resulting in the collapse of our society's norms and standards. The middle classes must reinstate themselves as arbiters of morality, be unafraid to judge their fellow men, and follow through with the condemnation that follows when individuals sin against common values.

'[Deane] thinks there is still an element in the population which has traditional middle-class values. Well, maybe.' **George Wedd**, *Contemporary Review*

£8.95/$17.90, 9780907845973 (pbk), *Societas* V.16

Who's Afraid of a European Constitution?
Neil MacCormick

This book discusses how the EU Constitution was drafted, whether it promises any enhancement of democracy in the EU, whether it implies that the EU is becoming a superstate, and whether it will strengthen the principle of subsidiarity and the protection of human rights.

Sir Neil MacCormick is professor of public law at Edinburgh University. He was an MEP and a member of the Convention on the Future of Europe.

'Those with a passing curiosity should find [the book] informative. Those already familiar… should find it entertaining and thought provoking.' *Scolag Legal J.*

£8.95/$17.90, 9781845392 (pbk), *Societas* V.17

Darwinian Conservatism
Larry Arnhart

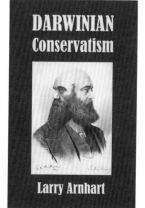

The Left has traditionally assumed that human nature is so malleable, so perfectible, that it can be shaped in almost any direction. Conservatives object, arguing that social order arises not from rational planning but from the spontaneous order of instincts and habits. Darwinian biology sustains conservative social thought by showing how the human capacity for spontaneous order arises from social instincts and a moral sense shaped by natural selection. The author is professor of political science at Northern Illinois University.

'Strongly recommended.' *Salisbury Review*

'An excellent book.' **Anthony Flew**, *Right Now!*

'Conservative critics of Darwin ignore Arnhart at their own peril.' *Review of Politics*

96 pp., £8.95/$17.90, 9780907845997 (pbk.), *Societas,* Vol. 18

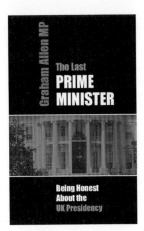

The Last Prime Minister
Graham Allen MP

This book shows how Britain has acquired an executive presidency by stealth. It is the first ever attempt to codify the Prime Minister's powers, many hidden in the mysteries of the royal prerogative. This timely second edition takes in new issues, including Parliament's impotence over Iraq.

'Iconoclastic, stimulating and well-argued.' **Vernon Bogdanor**, *Times Higher Education Supplement*

'Well-informed and truly alarming.' **Peter Hennessy**

'Should be read by anybody interested in the constitution.' **Anthony King**

£8.95/$17.90, 9780907845416 (pbk), *Societas* V.4

Doing Less With Less: Britain More Secure
Paul Robinson

Notwithstanding the rhetoric of the 'war on terror', the world is now a far safer place. However, armed forces designed for the Cold War encourage global interference through pre-emption and other forms of military interventionism. We would be safer with less. The author, an ex-army officer, is assistant director of the Centre for Security Studies at Hull University.

'Robinson's criticisms need to be answered.' **Tim Garden**, *RUSI Journal*

'The arguments in this thesis are important and should be acknowledged by the MOD.' **Major General (Retd.) Patrick Cordingley DSO**

£8.95/$17.90, 9781845400422 (pbk), *Societas* V.19

The Snake that Swallowed its Tail
Mark Garnett

Liberal values are the hallmark of a civilised society, but depend on an optimistic view of the human condition, Stripped of this essential ingredient, liberalism has become a hollow abstraction. Tracing its effects through the media, politics and the public services, the book argues that hollowed-out liberalism has helped to produce our present discontent. Garnett is the co-author of *The Essential A-Z Guide to Modern British History*.

'This arresting account will be read with profit by anyone interested in the role of ideas in politics.' **John Gray**, *New Statesman*

'A spirited polemic addressing the malaise of British politics.' **Michael Freeden**, *The European Legacy*

£8.95/$17.90, 9780907845881 (pbk), *Societas* V.12

The Party's Over
Keith Sutherland

This book questions the role of the party in the post-ideological age and concludes that government ministers should be appointed by headhunters and held to account by a parliament selected by lot.

'Sutherland's model of citizen's juries ought to have much greater appeal to progressive Britain.' *Observer*

'An extremely valuable contribution.' *Tribune*

'A political essay in the best tradition – shrewd, erudite, polemical, partisan, mischievous and highly topical.' *Contemporary Political Theory*

£8.95/$17.90, 9780907845515 (pbk), *Societas* V.10

Democracy, Fascism & the New World Order
Ivo Mosley

Growing up as the grandson of Sir Oswald, the 1930s blackshirt leader, made Ivo Mosley consider fascism with a deep and acutely personal interest. Whereas conventional wisdom sets up democracy and fascism as opposites, to ancient political theorists democracy had an innate tendency to lead to extreme populist government, and provided unscrupulous demagogues with the ideal opportunity to seize power. In *Democracy, Fascism and the New World Order* Mosley argues that totalitarian regimes may well be the logical outcome of unfettered mass democracy.

'Brings a passionate reasoning to the analysis'. *Daily Mail*

£8.95/$17.90, 9780907845645 (pbk), *Societas* V.6

The Case Against the Democratic State
Gordon Graham

This essay contends that the gross imbalance of power in the modern state is in need of justification and that democracy simply masks this need with the illusion of popular sovereignty. The book points out the emptiness of slogans like 'power to the people', as individual votes do not affect the outcome of elections, but concludes that democracy can contribute to civic education.

'Challenges the reigning orthodoxy'. *Mises Review*

'Political philosophy in the best analytic tradition... scholarly, clear, and it does not require a professional philosopher to understand it' *Philosophy Now*

'An excellent candidate for inclusion on an undergraduate syllabus.' *Independent Review*

£8.95/$17.90, 9780907845386 (pbk), *Societas* V.3

Off With Their Wigs!

Charles Banner and Alexander Deane

On June 12, 2003, a press release concerning a Cabinet reshuffle declared as a footnote that the ancient office of Lord Chancellor was to be abolished and that a new supreme court would replace the House of Lords as the highest appeal court. This book critically analyses the Government's proposals and looks at the various alternative models for appointing judges and for a new court of final appeal.

'A cogently argued critique.' *Commonwealth Lawyer*

£8.95/$17.90, 9780907845843 (pbk), *Societas* V.7

Universities: The Recovery of an Idea

Gordon Graham

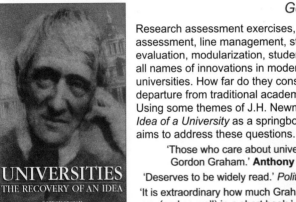

Research assessment exercises, teaching quality assessment, line management, student course evaluation, modularization, student fees – these are all names of innovations in modern British universities. How far do they constitute a significant departure from traditional academic concerns? Using some themes of J.H. Newman's classic *The Idea of a University* as a springboard, this book aims to address these questions.

'Those who care about universities should thank Gordon Graham.' **Anthony O'Hear**, *Philosophy*

'Deserves to be widely read.' *Political Studies Review*

'It is extraordinary how much Graham has managed to say (and so well) in a short book.' **Alasdair MacIntyre**

136 pp. *Societas*, Vol.1, subscription (retail edn: 9781845401009, £14.95/$29.90)

The Liberty Option

Tibor R. Machan

The Liberty Option advances the idea that it is the society organised on classical liberal principles that serves justice best, leads to prosperity and encourages the greatest measure of individual virtue. The book contrasts this Lockean ideal with the various statist alternatives, defends it against its communitarian critics and lays out some of its more significant policy implications. The author teaches ethics at Chapman University. His books on classical liberal theory include *Classical Individualism* (Routledge, 1998).

'The arguments are anchored largely in American politics, but have a wider resonance. A good read.' *Commonwealth Lawyer*

£8.95/$17.90, 9780907845638 (pbk), *Societas* V.5

Self and Society
William Irwin Thompson

The book is a series of essays on the evolution of culture, dealing with topics including the city and consciousness, evolution of the afterlife, literary and mathematical archetypes, machine consciousness and the implications of 9/11 and the invasion of Iraq for the development of planetary culture. The author is a poet, cultural historian and founder of the Lindisfarne Association. His sixteen books include *Coming into Being: Artifacts and Texts in the Evolution of Consciousness*.

£8.95/$17.90, 9780907845829 (pbk), *Societas* V.9

The Modernisation Imperative
Bruce Charlton & Peter Andras

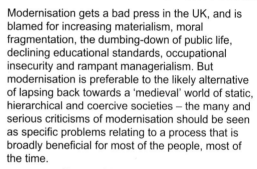

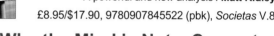

Modernisation gets a bad press in the UK, and is blamed for increasing materialism, moral fragmentation, the dumbing-down of public life, declining educational standards, occupational insecurity and rampant managerialism. But modernisation is preferable to the likely alternative of lapsing back towards a 'medieval' world of static, hierarchical and coercive societies – the many and serious criticisms of modernisation should be seen as specific problems relating to a process that is broadly beneficial for most of the people, most of the time.

'A powerful and new analysis'. **Matt Ridley**

£8.95/$17.90, 9780907845522 (pbk), *Societas* V.8

Why the Mind is Not a Computer
Raymond Tallis

The equation 'Mind = Machine' is false. This pocket lexicon of 'neuromythology' shows why. Taking a series of keywords such as calculation, language, information and memory, Professor Tallis shows how their misuse has a misled a generation. First of all these words were used literally in the description of the human mind. Then computer scientists applied them metaphorically to the workings of machines. And finally the use of the terms was called as evidence of artificial intelligence in machines *and* the computational nature of thought. .

'A splendid exception to the helpless specialisation of our age' **Mary Midgley**, *THES*

'A work of radical clarity.' *J. Consciousness Studies*

£8.95/$17.90, 9780907845942 (pbk), *Societas* V.13

Our Last Great Illusion

Rob Weatherill

This book aims to refute, primarily through the prism of modern psychoanalysis and postmodern theory, the notion of a return to nature, to holism, or to a pre-Cartesian ideal of harmony and integration. Far from helping people, therapy culture's utopian solutions may be a cynical distraction, creating delusions of hope. Yet solutions proliferate in the free market; this is why therapy is our last great illusion. The author is a psychoanalytic psychotherapist and lecturer, Trinity College, Dublin.

'Challenging, but well worth the engagement.' *Network*

£8.95/$17.90, 9780907845959 (pbk), *Societas* V.11

God in Us: A Case for Christian Humanism

Anthony Freeman

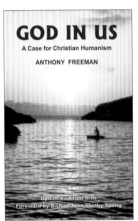

God In Us is a radical representation of the Christian faith for the 21st century. Following the example of the Old Testament prophets and the first-century Christians it overturns received ideas about God. God is not an invisible person 'out there' somewhere, but lives in the human heart and mind as 'the sum of all our values and ideals' guiding and inspiring our lives.

The Revd. Anthony Freeman was dismissed from his parish for publishing this book, but remains a priest in the Church of England.

'Brilliantly lucid.' *Philosophy Now*
'A brave and very well-written book' *The Freethinker*

£8.95/$17.90, 9780907845171 (pbk), *Societas* V.2

Societas: Essays in Political and Cultural Criticism

The books in this pamphlet are available retail at the price of £8.95/$17.90 from your local bookshop, or using the order form in the main Imprint Academic catalogue, or online at **imprint-academic.com/books**. See also our larger catalogue of monographs, collected essays and periodicals in philosophy, politics, psychology and cultural and religious studies.

However you can obtain the current volume (and back issues) on bi-monthly subscription for only £5/$10, using the direct debit form on the back of this brochure. Updates at **imprint-academic.com/societas** (overseas readers can subscribe via our credit card direct debit scheme.)

IMPRINT ACADEMIC, PO Box 200, Exeter, EX5 5HY, UK
Tel: (0)1392 851550   Fax: (0)1392 851178   sandra@imprint.co.uk

Cover painting: 'The Tryst' by John B. Harris

To qualify for the Direct Debit subscription rate, we will debit your account £5.00/$10.00 when each new book is despatched (every two months). We will supply you with details of the next title at the same time, so if you want to unsubscribe you can cancel the mandate at any time.

☐ Please register my *Societas* subscription, starting with the current title (see month of publication on p. 2–6 or at **imprint-academic.com/societas**). I would also like to order the following backlist titles for **only £2.50/$5.00 each.**

. . . .

. . . .

. . . .

IMPRINT ACADEMIC

Instruction to your Bank or Building Society to pay by Direct Debit

Please fill in the form and send to Imprint Academic, PO Box 200, Exeter EX5 5YX

To: The Manager   Bank/Building Society

Address

Originator's Identification Number

6 | 3 | 0 | 4 | 9 | 4

Reference

Name(s) of Account Holder(s)

Postcode

Branch Sort Code

Bank/Building Society account number

Instruction to your Bank or Building Society

Please pay Imprint Academic Direct Debits from the account detailed in this Instruction subject to the safeguards assured by the Direct Debit Guarantee. I understand that this instruction may remain with Imprint Academic and, if so, details will be passed electronically to my Bank/Building Society.

Signature(s)

Date

Banks and Building Societies may not accept Direct Debit Instructions for some types of account

DDI5

Name. . . . .

Address * . . . .

. . . .

Home telephone . . . . E-mail . . . . . .

Send completed form to Imprint Academic, PO Box 200, Exeter EX5 5HY, UK